Birdhouses
and Feeders

G. Barquest, S. Craven and R. Ellarson

DOVER PUBLICATIONS, INC.
Mineola, New York

Bibliographical Note

This Dover edition, first published in 2007, is an unabridged republication of *Shelves, Houses and Feeders for Birds and Mammals,* North Central Regional Extension Publication No. 338, originally published by the University of Wisconsin Cooperative Extension, Madison, Wisconsin in cooperation with the Extension Service of the U.S. Department of Agriculture, Washington, D.C., n.d.

Library of Congress Cataloging-in-Publication Data

Barquest, G.
    [Shelves, houses and feeders for birds and mammals]
    Birdhouses and feeders / G. Barquest, S. Craven, and R. Ellarson.
        p. cm.
    Previously published: Shelves, houses and feeders for birds and mammals.
Madison, Wisconsin : University of Wisconsin Cooperative Extension.
    Includes bibliographical references and index.
    ISBN-13: 978-0-486-46046-8 (pbk.)
    ISBN-10: 0-486-46046-0 (pbk.)
      1. Birdhouses. 2. Bird feeders. 3. Mammals—Housing. I. Craven, S. II. Ellarson, R. III. Title.

QL676.5.B266 2007
690'.8927—dc22

                                2007003353

Manufactured in the United States of America
Dover Publications, Inc., 31 East 2nd Street, Mineola, N.Y. 11501

CONTENTS *₰* CONTENTS *₰* CONTENTS

A REWARDING ACTIVITY

The study of birds and other wildlife is one of the fastest growing outdoor activities in this country today. Anyone can participate. There are no age limitations.

One of the most rewarding aspects of this activity is attracting wildlife to where they can be conveniently seen and studied. Ways in which this can be done depend on the kinds of animals we are interested in attracting.

Nesting and dwelling houses encourage certain birds and mammals to take up residence, while food can be used to attract most wintering birds.

Attracting and studying wildlife becomes doubly satisfying when we build the houses, shelters and feeders and then see how they are used by wildlife.

There are an amazing number of different designs and types of such structures, but the basic requirements are few.

They should provide for animals' safety and comfort, and they must be located in an area that will be attractive to the animals for which they were designed. If they are improperly located in relation to the needs and habits of the animals, they will go unused.

The demand for lumber and firewood, land development and changes in fence and building construction have reduced the number of nesting sites available for cavity-dependent birds and mammals. You can help many desirable species by providing nest structures.

Bird house and feeder construction can be an excellent project for school classes, FFA, Scouts, 4-H, conservation clubs and other groups. The finished products can be installed for public service projects, used as gifts, or sold as a fund-raiser.

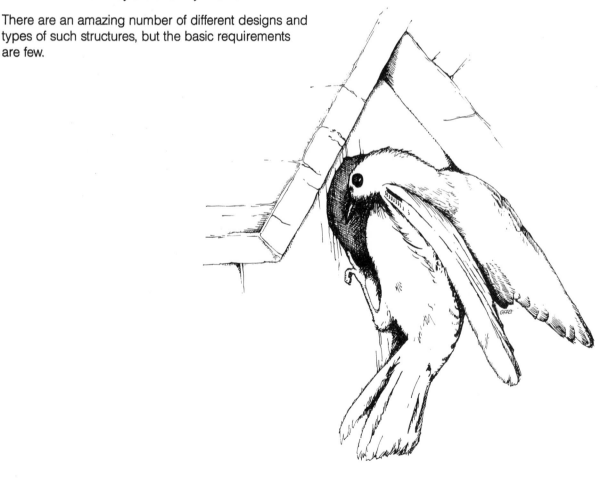

CONSTRUCTION GUIDELINES

The structures for birds and squirrels in this publication were designed with attractiveness, space requirements and efficient use of modern materials in mind. They provide ventilation, drainage and easy cleaning (nest houses should be cleaned each fall to protect young birds from lice and mites). You may increase inside dimensions slightly, but do not decrease them.

MATERIALS

A list of generally available materials is provided for each house or feeder. Lumber dimensions are given in standard "full-inch" sizes, but in reality the lumber you purchase will be thinner and narrower. (A 1 × 8 board is actually about 3/4 inch thick and 7¼ inches wide.) Where specified dimensions contain no inch marks ("), we are referring to the "nominal" lumber dimensions. Where inch marks are used, we are giving actual measurements.

Most kinds of lumber are satisfactory as long as the recommended sizes are used. Heartwoods of redwood and cedar are decay-resistant. However, they are expensive and have a tendency to split when nails are driven into short pieces without predrilled nail holes. (A nail with the head cut off may be used as a drill bit.)

Pine and spruce are more susceptible to decay than redwood and cedar, but they should last at least 6 to 10 years. Of the four woods mentioned, pine is the most split-resistant. Number 2 or 3 grades of either pine or spruce are the most economical overall and are generally satisfactory. Some spruce boards that are rough on one side and smooth on the other are available. The knots in these woods are not objectionable, and the wood may be assembled with either the smooth or rough side out.

Exterior grade 1/2" or 3/4" plywood may be used in place of lumber with a nominal thickness of 1 inch. (Actual measurements are used to express plywood thicknesses.) Plywood intended for sheathing and underlayment is not a suitable substitute for exterior grade because the plies may separate when it is completely exposed to the weather.

WOOD PRESERVATIVES AND TREATED WOOD

Do not use wood treated with creosote or pentachlorophenol (penta). We don't recommend using wood treated with greenish water-borne salts either because it is not yet known whether it may be harmful to wildlife. This type of wood preservative contains a combination of copper, chromium and arsenic.

ASSEMBLY

We recommend rust-resistant nails and screws. Galvanized 7d or 2¼" siding nails and galvanized 3d or 1¼" shingle nails are available at most hardware stores and lumber yards. Some stores also stock aluminum and stainless steel nails. Zinc-plated or zinc chromate-treated screws are rust-resistant.

Use only waterproof glue. We recommend liquid resorcinol with catalyst. Wood pieces may be held together with clamps or nails while the glue cures.

EXTERIOR FINISHES

A wide selection of exterior finishes is available. But the finish selected may please the maker more than the occupant. Unfinished structures made of redwood or cedar heartwood, pine, spruce or plywood will turn gray and last for years. Wood weathers away at the rate of about 1/4" per hundred years.

If you want a colored structure, semi-transparent oil-base stains commonly used on homes, resorts and fences are the most practical because they penetrate into wood without forming a film on the surface. They will not blister, crack, peel or scale even if moisture penetrates the wood. One application will last 3 years on smooth surfaces and 5 years on rough surfaces. Select a stain that does not contain pentachlorophenol preservative.

Latex stain can be used in place of an oil-base stain, but it is less durable. A workable latex stain can be prepared by diluting 1 part of exterior latex paint with 2 parts of water.

If you prefer a painted surface, treat it with a water-repellent solution and let it dry for a day or two before applying the primer. Use an oil-base primer and two top coats of acrylic latex house paint.

SHELVES

Robins and phoebes will not nest in enclosed nest boxes. However, they both readily use platforms or shelves in sheltered areas around buildings. One favored spot is under the eaves of buildings where they are protected by the overhang. Allow 6″ to 7″ clearance from the shelf to the overhang for robins and 4″ to 5″ clearance for phoebes.

Nesting platforms for robins may also be mounted on the trunk or main branches of a tree.

NEST SHELF FOR ROBINS AND PHOEBES

MATERIALS
1 piece 1 × 6 (about 3/4″ × 5½″) × 18″
1 piece 1 × 2 (about 3/4″ × 1½″) × 10″
8 1¾″ or 2¼″ nails

MOUNTING

Attach to the side of a building at least 10′ to 12′ above the ground in the shelter of the eaves or on the main branch of a tree in a shaded area.

ROOFED SHELF FOR ROBINS AND PHOEBES

MATERIALS

1 piece 1 × 10 (about 3/4″ × 9¼″) × 30″
1 piece 1 × 2 (about 3/4″ × 1½″) × 36″
1¾″ or 2¼″ nails
1¼″ nails

MOUNTING

Use roundhead or lag screws to mount on the south or east side of a building or in a tree at least 10′ to 12′ above the ground.

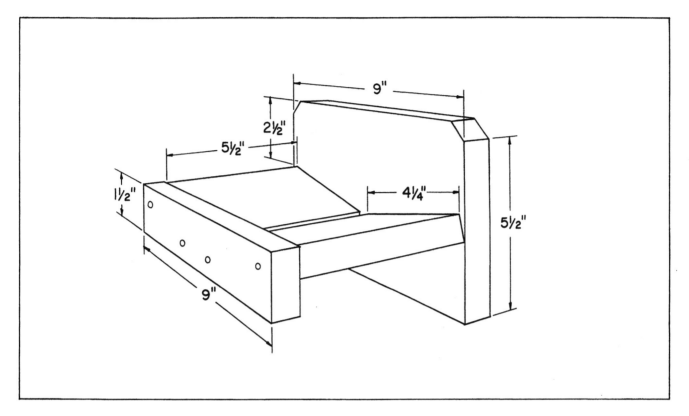

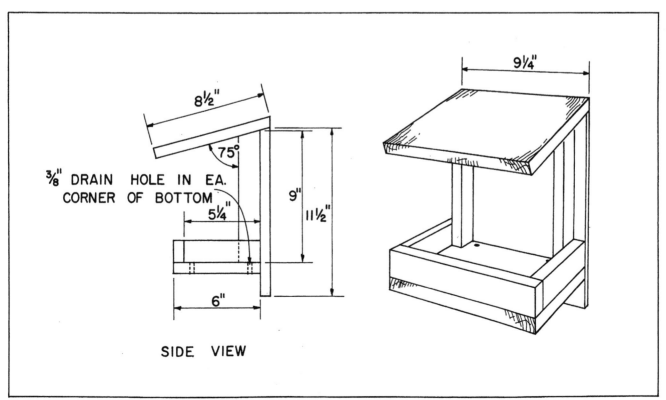

⅜" DRAIN HOLE IN EA.
CORNER OF BOTTOM

SIDE VIEW

HOUSES FOR WRENS, BLUEBIRDS AND TREE SWALLOWS

Wrens, bluebirds and tree swallows are the birds most commonly attracted to single-unit, enclosed bird houses. Each species prefers certain locations and habitats in which to nest and rear its young.

WRENS PREFER THICK COVER

To attract house wrens, place the box very close to or actually in the cover of a bush or small tree. Wrens seek the shade and protection of thick bushes where mated pairs find nesting materials and food for themselves and their young. The box may be placed 3' to 10' from the ground. In our university studies we placed wren boxes at about 5'. If cover is available, wrens will nest as high as 15' from the ground.

BLUEBIRDS CHOOSE FENCEROWS

Bluebirds and tree swallows are more exacting. Bluebirds will tolerate a shaded box but usually choose fairly open areas interspersed with trees and shrubs. Place bluebird boxes 4' to 6' above the ground. The bluebird is truly a bird of the fencerow, preferring cavities of rotted wooden fence posts. In recent years, bluebird numbers have greatly diminished, but in some localities well-placed nest boxes along fencerows or in orchards have helped this handsome species maintain its numbers.

TREE SWALLOWS SEEK THE OPEN

The tree swallow feeds on the wing and seeks open agricultural fields and meadows or treeless and shrubless wild areas as its nesting place. A nest box for the tree swallow must be placed in the open on a fence post or special box support. A broad sweep of open country in front of the box opening is the best inducement for the tree swallow to accept the box. This graceful swallow is not particular about the height of its nest cavity, provided the above requirements are met. We recommend placing tree swallow boxes 5' to 6' above the ground.

NESTING MATERIAL VARIES

The wren builds the bulk of its nest of sticks, the bluebird uses grass, and the tree swallow gathers large chicken, duck or gamebird feathers to line a shallow nest of grass and roots. Usually there is no lack of these materials in the wild, but we have encouraged tree swallows and wrens to use our boxes by placing nesting material near the boxes.

SPACE THE BOXES

Spacing of boxes is necessary because birds space themselves naturally during the nesting period. Some birds, such as purple martins, gulls, cliff swallows or ledge-nesting sea birds, will tolerate other nests at very close quarters. But others—hawks, owls, kingbirds, and even robins—cannot be crowded into small spaces, nor can you get wrens to nest together in a house like martins.

The spacing of nest boxes depends on the arrangement of the food and cover and the degree of isolation this arrangement affords. In general, the average city back yard or garden is large enough for one or perhaps two families of wrens. The large expanses required for tree swallows and bluebirds eliminates these birds from most city locations. In farm yards or in rural areas, a tree swallow box should be at least 30 feet away from any other box. Bluebird spacing is less critical than that for tree swallows, but a box every 150 feet should be adequate.

Put the bird boxes up by March 15 so they will be ready when the birds arrive from the South. Occasionally, unwanted birds like the English sparrow or European starlings take over boxes. You can discourage them by repeatedly removing their nests. A periodic check will tell you if you have desirable tenants to encourage or undesirable ones to evict.

It often takes several boxes placed in the most likely sites to attract one pair of birds.

WREN HOUSE

MATERIALS

1 piece 1 × 6 (about 3/4″ × 5½″) × 24″
1 piece 1 × 4 (about 3/4″ × 3½″) × 12″
Use box lumber, bevel siding, exterior plywood, heavy
    asphalt roofing or tin for roof.
4 roundhead wood screws to attach one side of roof
9 1¾″ or 2¼″ nails
8 1¼″ nails

CONSTRUCTION

Attach one side of roof with wood screws, so it can be
removed for annual house cleaning.

MOUNTING

Attach to a tree or post 5′ to 6′ above ground with
roundhead or lag screws.

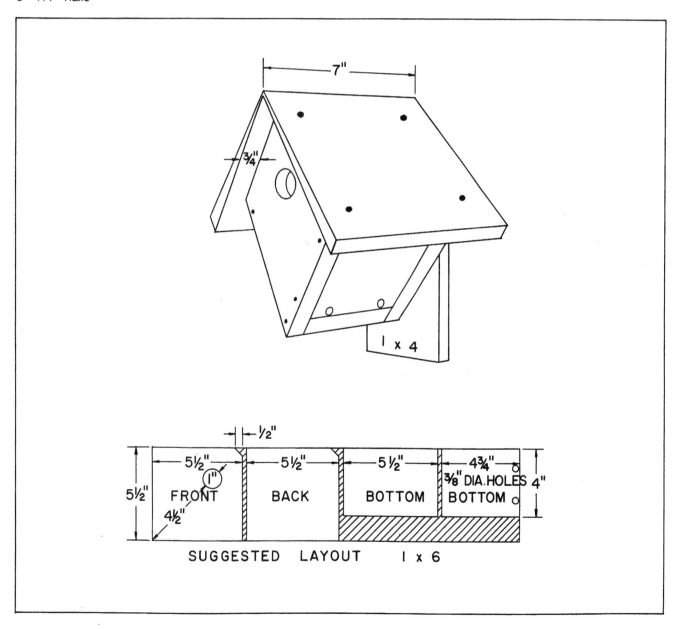

SUGGESTED LAYOUT   1 × 6

HOUSE FOR WRENS, BLUEBIRDS, TREE SWALLOWS

MATERIALS

1 piece 1 × 6 (about 3/4″ × 5½″) × 54″
1 piece 3/4″ × 10″ × 8″ bevel siding or other
   material for roof
1 piece 1 × 4 (about 3/4″ × 3½″) × 4″ for coon or
   starling guard
3   1½″ #10 roundhead wood screws
1¼″ nails—roof and guard
1¾″ or 2¼″ nails

CONSTRUCTION

1. Drill 3/8″ diameter drain hole in each corner of the
   bottom.

2. Hinged side should be 1/16″ shorter than the other
   side.

3. Drill holes in front and back pieces slightly larger
   than shank of pivot screws.

MOUNTING

Attach to a tree or post 5′ to 6′ above ground with
roundhead or lag screws through the bottom of the
back piece.

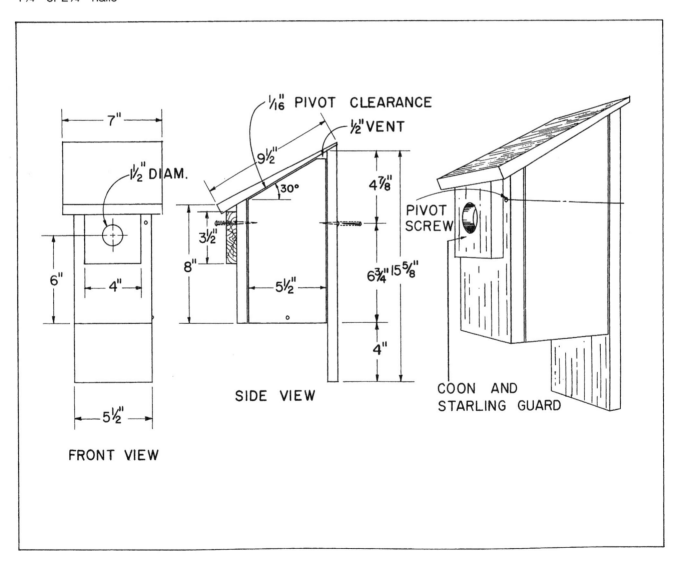

TIN CAN HOUSE

MATERIALS

1 can about 7″ tall and 6″ in diameter
1 piece 1 × 8 (about 3/4″ × 7¼″) × 10″ or
   equivalent 1/2″ or 3/4″ exterior grade plywood
1 piece 1 × 2 (about 3/4″ × 1½″) × 10″ for diagonal
   cleat. (May be omitted if plywood is used for roof)
2 screw eyes
1 piece of 11 gauge wire 8″ long. A section of wire
   clothes hanger may be substituted
4 1¼″ galvanized nails to attach cleat

FINISH

Wash can with vinegar, allow to dry, then wash with
clean water and allow to dry. Paint with a good grade
exterior house paint, metal paint or enamel. Use metal
primer if available.

MOUNTING

Attach to a fence post or tree trunk with stove pipe wire
or similar size wire.

NOTE: While ventilation is important for all bird houses,
it is especially important with the tin can design. *Do
not* overlook the vent holes.

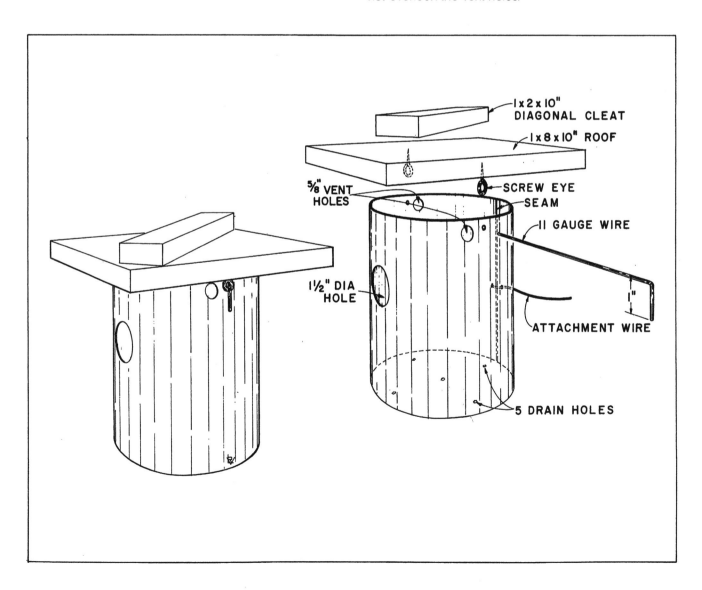

BLUEBIRD HOUSES

The Bluebird Restoration Association of Wisconsin has been instrumental in the recovery of Wisconsin bluebird populations. For more information about the association, contact the BRAW coordinator in your Wisconsin county or the Wisconsin Department of Natural Resources, Bureau of Endangered Resources, Box 7921, Madison, WI 53707. The following house designs are recommended by BRAW.

VINCE BAULDRY BLUEBIRD HOUSE

MATERIALS AND CONSTRUCTION

1. Front: Wood—3/4″ × 5½″ × 14″ (Std. 6″ board)

2. Front: Wood—1½″ × 3½″ × 4½″ (Std. 2″ × 4″)

3. Top: Wood—3/4″ × 7¼″ × 8″ (Std. 8″ board) Hole 3½″ dia. located 2 7/8″ from back edge. Screen 5″ square held between wood. Tack in place before assembly.

4. Sides: Wood—3/4″ × 4″ × 14″. 2 needed. Locate left-hand side 1/8″ lower than other and nail only at top. Loose pin or nail will keep door closed.

5. Bottom: Wood—3/4″ × 4″ × 4″. Nail on three sides.

6. Back: Wood—3/4″ × 5½″ × 18″ (Std. 6″ board)

7. Nails: Galvanized, 1½″ long. 26 needed.

3/4″ Exterior plywood may be used.

Rough side of lumber to outside.

Leave exterior natural or paint with light shades of gray, beige or green. DO NOT paint interior or entry hole. Use wood stain or latex paint. Make 2 parallel saw cuts, 1/8″ deep, beneath the entry hole.

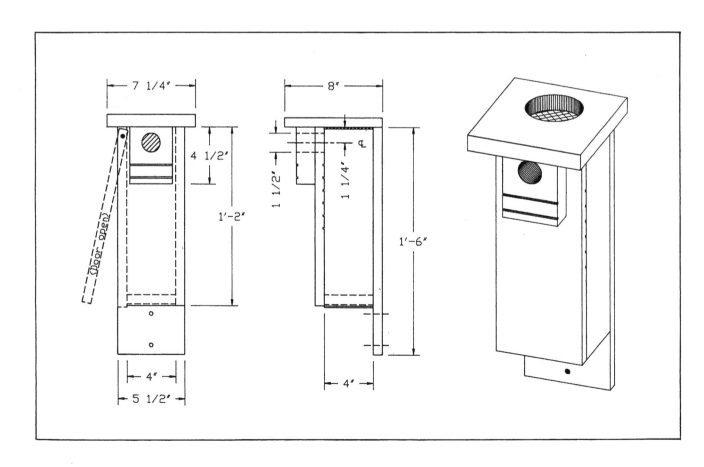

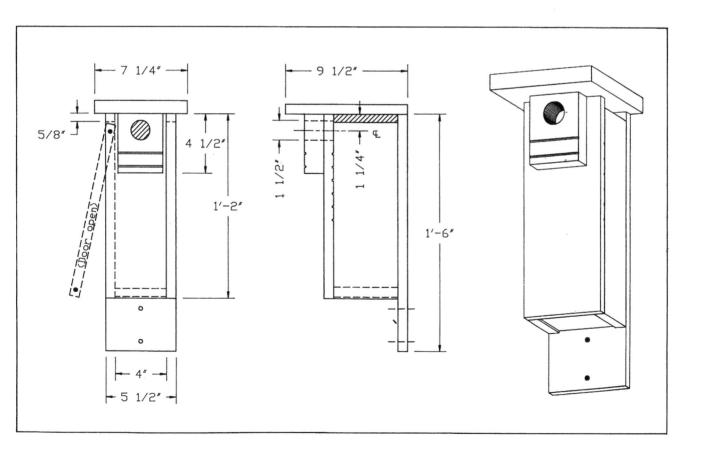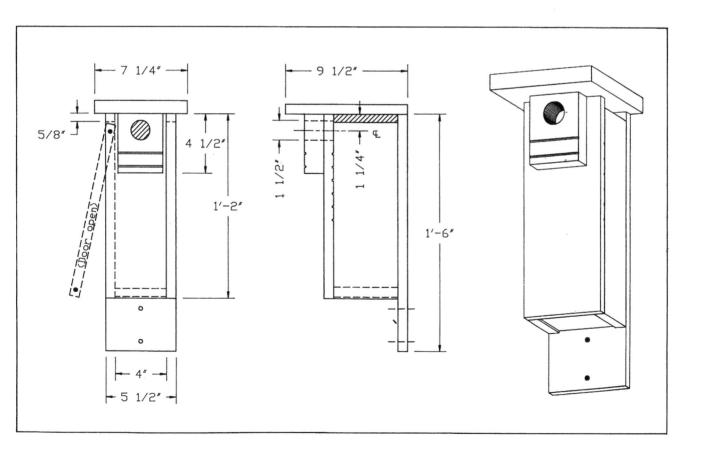
HILL LAKE BLUEBIRD HOUSE
(Using All Standard Lumber)

MATERIALS AND CONSTRUCTION

1. Front: Wood—3/4″ × 5½″ × 14″ (Std. 6″ board)

2. Front: Wood—1½″ × 3½″ × 4½″ (Std. 2 ″ × 4″).

3. Top: Wood—3/4″ × 7¼″ × 9½″ (Std. 8″ board)

4. Top: Wood—3/4″ × 5½″ × 13 3/8″ (Std. 6″ bd.).
   2 needed.
   Locate left hand side (access door) flush with bottom of front and nail only at top for pivot points. (5/8″ vent space above each side.) Loose pin or nail will keep door closed.

5. Bottom: Wood—3/4″ × 5½″ × 4″. (Std. 6″ bd.). Nail 3 sides.

6. Back: Wood—3/4″ × 5½″ × 18″. (Std. 6″ board)

Nails: Galvanized, 1½″ long. 26 needed.

3/4″ Exterior plywood may be used.

Rough side of lumber to outside.

Leave exterior natural or paint with light shades of gray, beige or green. DO NOT paint interior or entry hole. Use wood stain or latex paint. Make 2 parallel saw cuts 1/8″ deep, beneath the entry hole.

PETERSON BLUEBIRD HOUSE

MATERIALS AND CONSTRUCTION

1. Back: Wood—1½" × 3½" × 24"

2. Front: Wood—3/4" × 3 3/8 × 12½"

3. Inner Top: Wood—1½" × 3½" × 8 3/8"

4. Top: Wood—3/4" × 9¼" × 13"

5. Sides: Wood—3/4" × 10¼" × 2¾" × 17½" × 14 3/8"

6. Bottom: Wood—1½" × 3½" × 3"

7. Pegs: Wood—1/4" dia. × 2¼" long. (1½" Projection *inside*.)

Nails: Galvanized, 1½" long. 26 needed.

Rough side of lumber to outside.

3/4" Exterior plywood may be used.

Leave exterior natural or paint with light shades of gray, beige or green. DO NOT paint interior or entry hole. Use wood stain or latex paint. Make 2 parallel saw cuts 1/8" deep, beneath the entry hole.

All lumber is standard 1" (actually 3/4" thick) except BACK, INNER TOP and BOTTOM, which are standard 2" × 4" (actually 1½" × 3½").

DO NOT USE OUTSIDE PERCH!

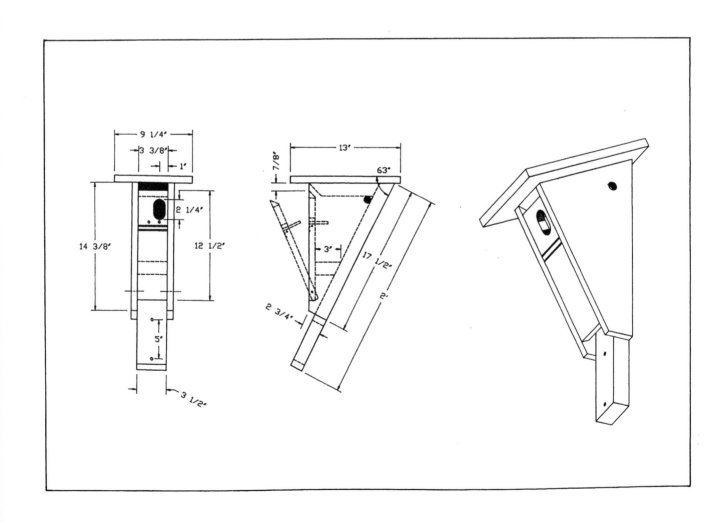

HERMAN OLSON BLUEBIRD HOUSE

MATERIALS AND CONSTRUCTION

1. Front: Wood—3/4″ × 6½″ × 10″

2. Front: Wood—3/4″ × 3½″ × 3½″

3. Top: Wood—3/4″ × 7¼″ × 9″

4. Sides: Wood—3/4″ × 5″ × 8½″ (short side); 3/4″ × 5″ × 9½″ (long side). 2 needed.
Locate left hand side (access door) flush with bottom of front and nail only at top for pivot points. (1/2″ vent space above each side.) Loose pin or nail will keep door closed.

5. Bottom: Wood—3/4″ × 5″ × 5″

6. Back: Wood—3/4″ × 6½″ × 14″

Nails: Galvanized, 1½″ long. 21 needed.

Rough side of lumber to outside.

3/4″ Exterior plywood may be used.

Leave exterior natural or paint with light shades of gray, beige or green. DO NOT paint interior or entry hole. Use wood stain or latex paint. Make 2 parallel saw cuts 1/8″ deep, beneath the entry hole.

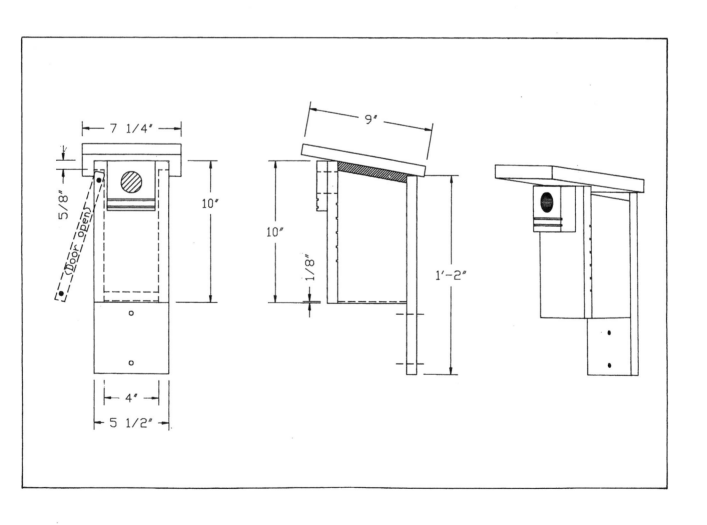

HOUSES FOR PURPLE MARTINS

A backyard colony of purple martins has become a status symbol. It is one status symbol, however, that cannot be purchased. Whether you are fortunate enough to have a colony rests with these handsome swallows themselves. But there are a number of things you can do to improve your chances of establishing a colony.

SELECT OPEN AREA

A martin house should be placed in an open area where the birds have clear access from all sides. Never place it where trees are closer than 30'. Martins like to perch on utility wires near their house. Houses near open water appear to have added appeal, but this is not essential.

Martin houses should be painted a light color to reflect the sun's heat and make the houses more comfortable for the birds. White is commonly used.

The height of the pole on which the house is mounted is important. A 12' to 15' pole is high enough in most open locations. Sixteen to 18 feet is better if buildings are nearby, and even taller poles may be used in areas having considerable shrub and small tree cover.

HOUSES SHOULD BE REMOVABLE

The pole should allow you to easily lower the house to the ground for winter storage, for cleaning and repairing or painting, and to prevent English sparrows and starlings from using it while the martins are gone.

Take the house down after the martins have left in fall (usually by September), and remove all old nesting material. Put it up shortly before the martins return in the spring. In Wisconsin this is usually the first week of April in the south, and somewhat later in the north.

PROTECT HOUSE FROM INTRUDERS

English sparrows and starlings compete with martins for nest houses, but you can discourage them by repeatedly destroying their nests. This will not cause the martins to abandon the house if you do the job with reasonable speed and care. Martins readily take to a variety of colony-type bird houses, and either the ranch type or conventional two-story house should be equally effective in attracting them. The style you build is up to you.

MARTIN HOUSE POLE

MATERIALS

1 piece 4 × 4 (about 3½" × 3½") × 8' CCA-treated wood rated for ground contact
1 piece 4 × 4 (about 3½" × 3½") × 10' CCA-treated wood rated for ground contact
1 piece 4 × 4 (about 3½" × 3½") × 12' to 18' CCA-treated wood rated for above-ground use
1 piece 1 × 4 (about 3/4" × 3½") × 4' CCA-treated wood rated for ground contact
1 1/2" × 24" or 36" threaded rod
4 1/2" steel washers
4 1/2" nuts
7d galvanized nails

POLE ASSEMBLY

1. The pole supports, pieces number 1 and 2, are 4 × 4 × 8'. They are held in a spread position by pieces (a) (4 × 4 × 6"), and nailed in place with pieces (b). The pole supports are set 4' in the ground.

2. The pole is hinged on the lower bolt.

3. It is also possible to build a 4¼" × 4¼" pole of four 1 × 4 boards.

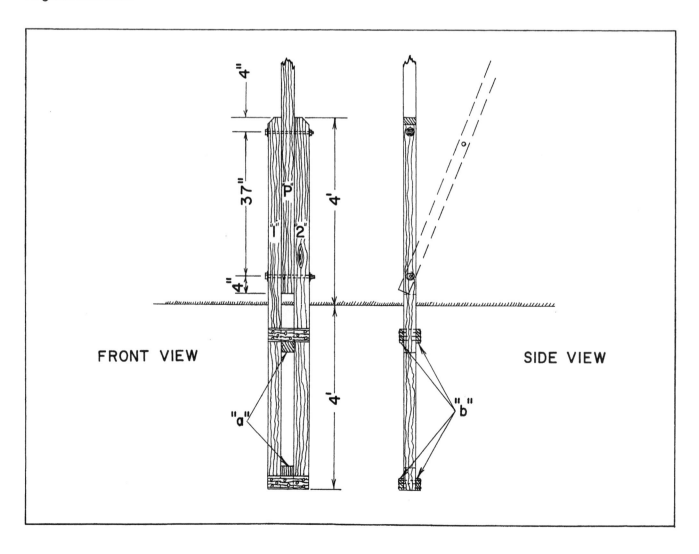

FRONT VIEW   SIDE VIEW

TWO-STORY
MARTIN HOUSE

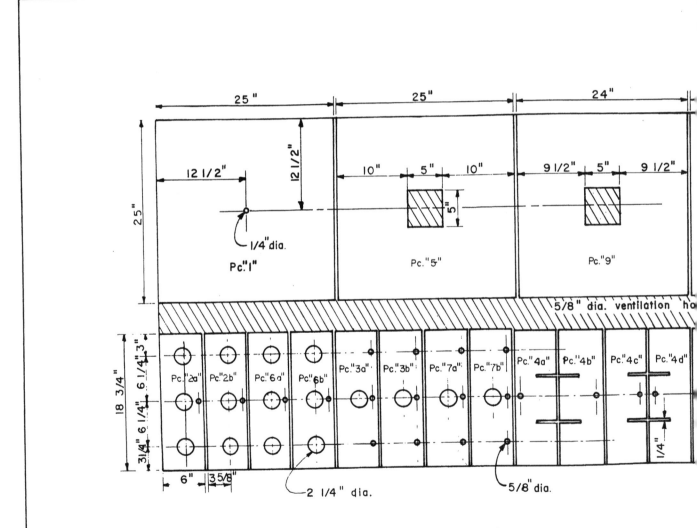

25" 25" 24"

12 1/2" 12 1/2" 10" 5" 10" 9 1/2" 5" 9 1/2"

25" 5" 5"

1/4" dia.

Pc."1" Pc."5" Pc."9"

5/8" dia. ventilation ho

18 3/4" 3" 6 1/4" 6 1/4" 6 1/4" 3/4"

Pc."2a" Pc."2b" Pc."6a" Pc."6b" Pc."3a" Pc."3b" Pc."7a" Pc."7b" Pc."4a" Pc."4b" Pc."4c" Pc."4d"

1/4"

6" 3 5/8"

2 1/4" dia. 5/8" dia.

LAYOUT FOR 4'x 8' SHEET

MATERIALS

1 sheet 4′ × 8′ exterior type 1/4″ plywood
1 sheet 2′ × 4′ exterior type 1/4″ plywood (with face grain in 2′ direction)
1 piece 2 × 2 (about 1½″ × 1½″) × 6″ for chimney
1 piece 1 × 2 (about 3/4″ × 1½″) × 14′ pine or spruce
1 piece 1 × 1 (about 3/4″ × 3/4″) × 8′ pine or spruce

1 piece 4″ × 8″ aluminum or copper window screen
Wire cloth staples
2″ or 2¼″ nails
1″ wire nails or 3/4″ #6 flathead screws (rust-resistant)
Resorcinol glue (waterproof)
1 each 1/4″ × 24″ or 30″ thread rod with 2 nuts and 2 washers

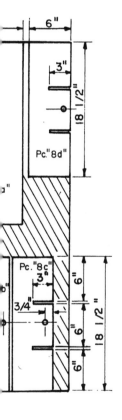

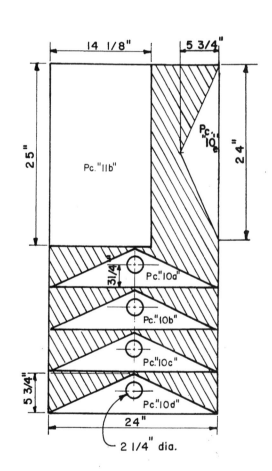

LAYOUT   FOR   2′ x 4′   SHEET

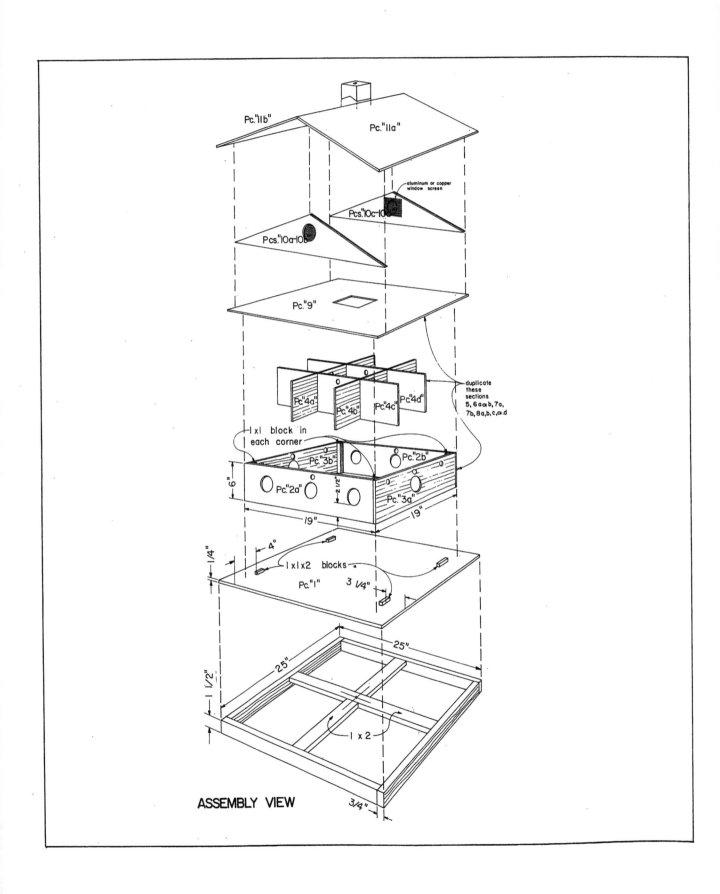

Pc."11b"

Pc."11a"

aluminum or copper
window screen

Pcs."10c-10d"

Pcs."10a-10b"

Pc."9"

duplicate
these
sections
5, 6 a a b, 7a,
7b, 8a,b,c,a.d

Pc."4a"

Pc."4b" Pc."4c" Pc."4d"

1 x 1 block in
each corner

Pc."3b"

Pc."2b"

6"

Pc."2a" 2 1/2"

Pc."3a"

19" 19"

1/4"

4"

1 x 1 x 2 blocks

Pc."1"

3 1/4"

25"

1 1/2" 25"

1 x 2

ASSEMBLY VIEW

3/4"

CONSTRUCTION

NOTE: This unit is held together by a thread rod extending from underside of 1 × 2 base frame through the center of the chimney.

1. Lay out all pieces on plywood sheets, then cut them out. Make eight 1 × 1 × 5 7/8" corner blocks and sixteen 1 × 1 × 2" blocks to position the parts.

2. Cut out and assemble base from 1 × 2. Use 7d galvanized siding nails. Attach piece 1 with glue and 1" or 1¼" nails.

3. Assemble sidewalls for first story (pieces 2a, 2b, 3a and 3b) and for second story (pieces 6a, 6b, 7a and 7b). Use glue and 1" nails or 3/4" #6 flathead wood screws. Use three at each end of each piece.

4. Position first-story sidewalls on base piece. Mark position for each 1 × 1 × 2" block to hold sidewall in position. Attach blocks to piece 1 with glue and two 1" nails or 3/4" #6 flathead wood screws. Place sidewall in position on piece 1. Insert partitions. Position piece 5 and mark for the location of 1 × 1 × 2" blocks near corners on the *underside.* Attach the blocks.

5. Place piece 5 in position. Position the second story sidewalls on piece 5, and mark for the location of the 1 × 1 × 2" blocks. Move them to the opposite side of the corner from the blocks underneath for convenience in attachment to piece 5. Attach blocks. Position sidewalls. Insert partitions.

6. Position piece 9. Mark location for 1 × 1 × 2" positioning blocks on *underside.* Attach blocks.

7. Glue pieces 10a, 10b, 10c and 10d together to form gable ends 1/2" thick. Attach screen. Position and mark. Glue scrap pieces to piece 10e to make it 1/2" thick. It will be positioned adjacent to the threaded rod going up through the exact center of the house. Attach these pieces with glue and nails or flathead wood screws from the underside. Attach roof pieces with glue and nails or screws.

8. Make chimney from a piece of 2 × 2. Cut V-notch on end to fit roof. Have it extend 2½" above roof peak. Drill 1/4" hole in chimney and roof for rod. Nail chimney in place. Insert rod and tighten up.

9. Drill hole in top of pole to accommodate nut on lower end of threaded rod.

MOUNTING

Use four 4" × 5" shelf brackets with 1/4" or 3/16" × 1½" roundhead stove bolts and 1" #8 flathead wood screws to attach to pole. See plans for ranch style martin house for pole detail and location.

NOTE: Additional stories may be added if desired.

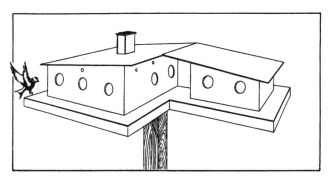

RANCH STYLE MARTIN HOUSE

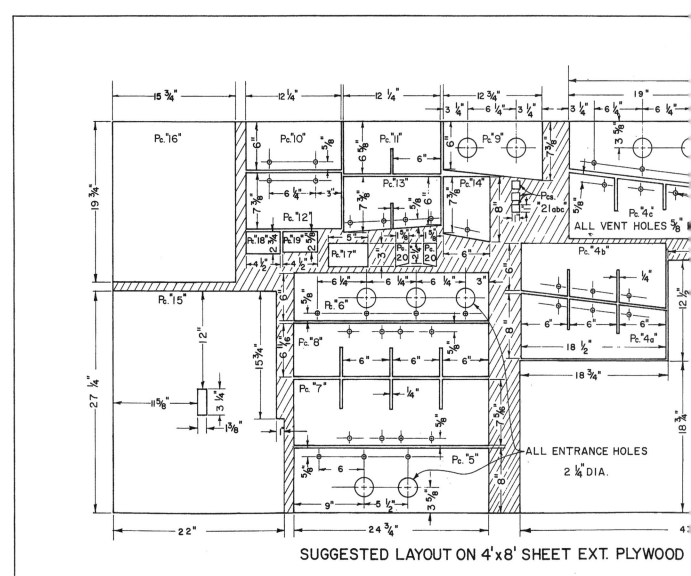

SUGGESTED LAYOUT ON 4'x8' SHEET EXT. PLYWOOD

MATERIALS

1 sheet 4′ × 8′ exterior type 1/4″ plywood
1 piece 1 × 4 (about 3/4″ × 3½″) × 4′ pine
1 piece 1 × 2 (about 3/4″ × 1½″) × 16′ pine
1 piece 1 × 1 (about 3/4″ × 3/4″) × 10′ pine
4 8″ × 10″ shelf brackets
12 1/4″ × 1/2″ flathead stove bolts
12 1¼″ #10 flathead wood screws
10 3/4″ #8 roundhead wood screws to attach roof

1¾″ or 2¼″ nails
1″ wire nails
Resorcinol glue
Paint

HOUSE ASSEMBLY

1. Use resorcinol glue for all joints. Use nails or clamps to hold pieces while the glue is setting.tir

2. Paint with a good exterior type house paint.

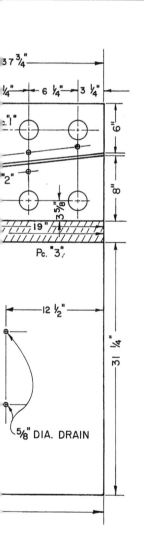

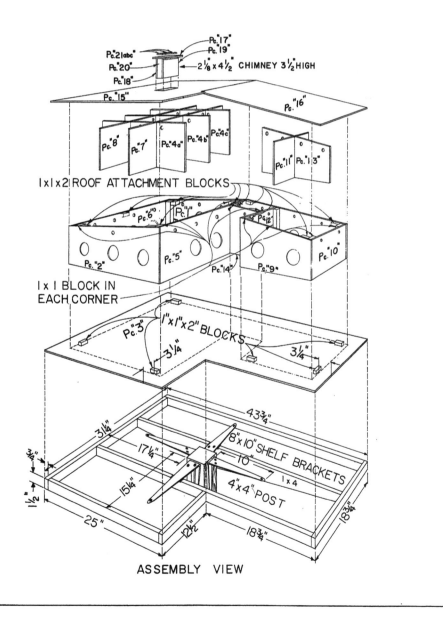

ASSEMBLY VIEW

HOUSES FOR SPARROW HAWKS AND SCREECH OWLS

Most people do not consider the possibility of attracting hawks and owls with houses. However, sparrow hawks (also called kestrels) and screech owls will readily use houses placed in suitable habitat.

Hawks and owls are highly territorial birds, so their nesting densities are low compared to songbirds'. Nevertheless, the satisfaction of attracting these birds to an area is well worth the effort of putting up several houses in likely spots. Sparrow hawks are our smallest true falcons. They are birds of open fields and meadows, where they hunt their prey—primarily meadow mice and insects such as grasshoppers. Locate houses on isolated living or dead trees, or possibly on poles. Houses should be at least 12' to 15' above the ground, with no obstructions in front of the hole. You are most likely to attract a nesting pair in areas where you've seen sparrow hawks perched on wires and feeding. Place an inch or two of coarse sawdust in the house before putting it up.

Screech owls are primarily woodland birds, and prefer houses in wooded areas. Attach the houses to trees 15' or more above the ground. The owls use the houses for shelter the year 'round, as well as for nesting sites during spring. During the winter they often sun themselves at the entrance hole, so nail a small cleat to the inside of the box 5" below the hole. Face the house so that the entrance will get the winter sun. Place several inches of sawdust or dry leaves in the house to make it more attractive.

SPARROW HAWK AND SCREECH OWL HOUSE

MATERIALS

1 piece 1 × 10 (about 3/4" × 9¼") × 4'
1 piece 1 × 8 (about 3/4" × 7¼") × 4'
1 piece 1 × 2 (about 3/4" × 1½") × 1' for cleat
1¾" or 2¼" nails
1¼" nails for roof section assembly
1 1¼" roundhead wood screw to attach roof

CONSTRUCTION

Use a piece of 1 × 10, with grain direction front to back, for roof. To reduce warping and keep the roof piece in position, attach a piece of 1 × 8, with grain direction side to side, on the underside. Reduce in size and slightly bevel the front edge of the 1 × 8 piece so it can be raised when the screw is removed. The 1 × 2 permanently attached cleat in the back and the screw in front keep the roof in place.

MOUNTING

Attach to tree trunk 12' to 30' above the ground. Use a lag screw and washer at both top and bottom of the back piece.

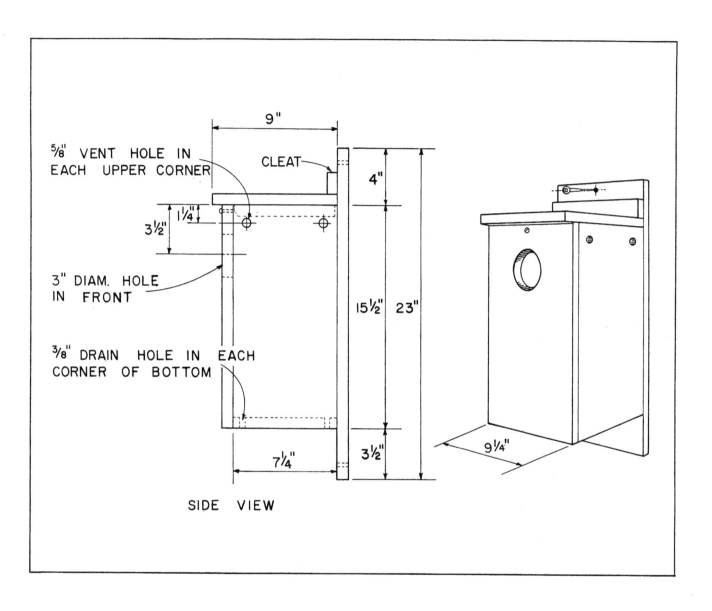

9"

⁵⁄₈" VENT HOLE IN
EACH UPPER CORNER

CLEAT

4"

3½"   1¼"

3" DIAM. HOLE
IN FRONT

15½"   23"

⅜" DRAIN HOLE IN EACH
CORNER OF BOTTOM

7¼"   3½"

SIDE VIEW

9¼"

BARN OWL HOUSING

Barn owls live throughout most of the United States. But their populations have declined in much of the Midwest, especially on the northern edge of their range. In Wisconsin barn owls are an endangered species. Most wildlife managers attribute this decline to a lack of secure nesting sites and changes in farming practices. Old, abandoned farms provided ideal nesting sites in lofts, rafters, and empty silos. Modern construction and materials do not provide such opportunities, but a well built, properly placed nest box can.

BARN OWL ECOLOGY

Barn owls—sometimes called "living mousetraps"—are very efficient predators of rodents. A barn owl may eat a dozen mice a night. To a farmer, there are real benefits to having barn owls around besides the satisfaction of helping a rare species.

Barn owls migrate south for the winter and usually return to Wisconsin in March. Their young hatch in May or June and are ready to leave by October. Adults generally stay in Wisconsin until early January, and may not leave at all during mild winters. Prior to human settlement, barn owls nested in large hollow trees, caves, or other natural cavities.

NEST BOX PLACEMENT

Barn owls are rather nervous and easily disturbed, so be sure to choose nest box sites that minimize potential disturbances. Unused barns, outbuildings, or silos are best. Church steeples and other obscure sites are also good. If you find evidence of previous use, such as regurgitated pellets or whitewash, that site is an excellent choice for a nest box. Place the nest box high on a wall or in a silo to protect the owls from marauding raccoons, cats or dogs.

IF YOU ATTRACT BARN OWLS...

If barn owls use your nest box, please write or call the Wisconsin Department of Natural Resources, Bureau of Endangered Resources, Box 7921, Madison, WI 53707; phone (608) 266-7012. Nesting information is very valuable and will help wildlife managers determine population status and better manage barn owls in the future.

BARN OWL NEST BOX

You can build the nest box from a 6-foot length of 1 × 12 pine board and 1/2" utility grade plywood, or entirely from 1/2" plywood. Materials and general dimensions of the box can vary depending upon materials available.

MATERIALS

1 bottom, 1 × 12 (about 3/4" × 11¼") × 40"—pine
2 ends, 1 × 12 × 16"—pine
1 back, 16" × 41½"—plywood
1 top, 11 3/4" × 41½"—plywood

       or

1 bottom, 12" × 40"—plywood
2 ends, each 12" × 16"—plywood
1 back, 16" × 41"—plywood
1 top, 12½" × 41"—plywood
7d or 8d box nails

MOUNTING

The barn wall acts as the front of the box. Nail the box together with 7d or 8d box nails. The top should be removable for cleaning the box but secured by hinges and a latch, or partially nailed in place, to keep raccoons out.

Mount the box on a cross beam against the inside wall of the barn after cutting a 6" × 6" hole above the beam. Entrance placement is important to prevent young owls from falling out of the box. Position the box with the entrance about 2 inches from one end and nail it securely to the cross beam, through the bottom of the box. If the beam is narrow, additional support under the box or a wire or rope extending from the lower corners of the box to the barn wall may be necessary.

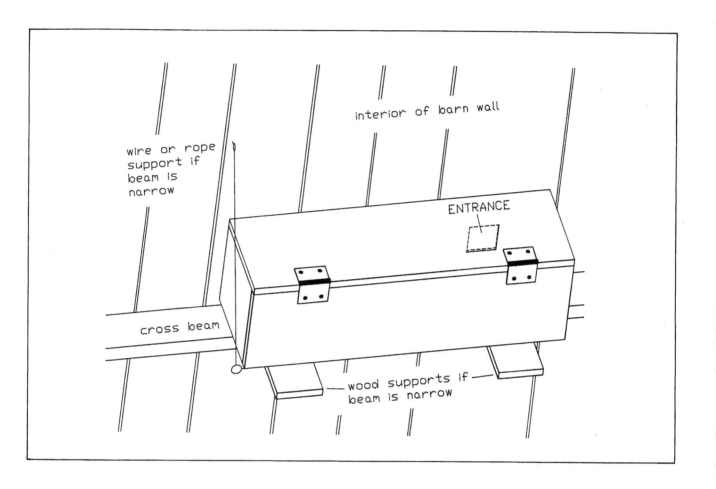

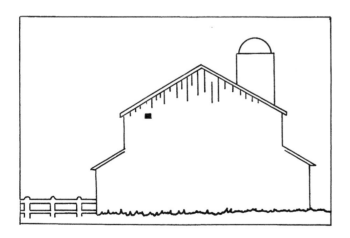

Nest box design and instructions courtesy of the Ohio Department of Natural Resources and the Wisconsin Department of Natural Resources.

HOUSES FOR WOOD DUCKS

Wood ducks, the most beautiful of all North American waterfowl, normally nest in hollow trees near marshes, lakes and streams. They readily take to man-made structures, and their population can be increased by providing suitable houses.

Erect houses in a wet marsh by attaching to a sturdy pole set 4' to 6' or more above high water level. Houses may also be placed in trees up to 1/4 mile from the water. When placed in a tree, the house should be 8' to 30' above the ground. Take care that the house is plainly visible and that the entrance hole is not obstructed by leaves and branches. The house should be in a vertical position, but if it slants it must be forward. A backward slant prevents the young from climbing the sides and leaving the house after hatching. Place three or four inches of coarse sawdust or shavings in the house when it is erected.

Raccoons and tree-climbing snakes prey on wood duck nests. Protect houses with suitable guards, such as metal shields around the tree trunk or post, wherever these animals are apt to present a problem.

Occasionally birds such as starlings, flickers and screech owls will take over wood duck houses, and squirrels may also occupy them. Check the houses periodically to evict undesirable tenants, or erect additional houses for the ducks.

WOOD DUCK HOUSE

MATERIALS

1 piece 1 × 12 (about 3/4″ × 11¼″) × 5'
1 piece 1 × 10 (about 3/4″ × 9¼″) × 6'
1 piece 1 × 2 (about 3/4″ × 1½″) × 1' for cleat
1¾″ or 2¼″ nails
1¼″ nails for roof section
1 1¼″ roundhead wood screw
1 piece 3″ × 12″, 1/4″ or 3/8″ mesh hardware cloth
   (see construction notes)
poultry netting staples (galvanized)

CONSTRUCTION

If inside surface of front board is smooth, attach a 3″ × 12″ strip of hardware cloth on the inside. Have it extend from the bottom of the hole down 12 inches. Saw cuts 1/8″ deep and 1/2″ apart in the same area are suitable.

Use a piece of 1 × 12, with the grain direction front to back, for roof. To reduce warping and to keep the roof piece in position, attach a piece of 1 × 10, with the grain direction side to side, on the underside. Reduce in size and slightly bevel the front edge of the 1 × 10 piece so it can be raised when the screw is removed. The 1 × 2 permanently attached cleat in the back and the screw in front keep the roof in place.

MOUNTING

Attach to tree trunk 8′ to 30′ above the ground where
no branches shield the entrance. It may also be
attached to a sturdy pole in shallow water just a few
feet above the water. Use a lag screw and washer at
both top and bottom of back piece.

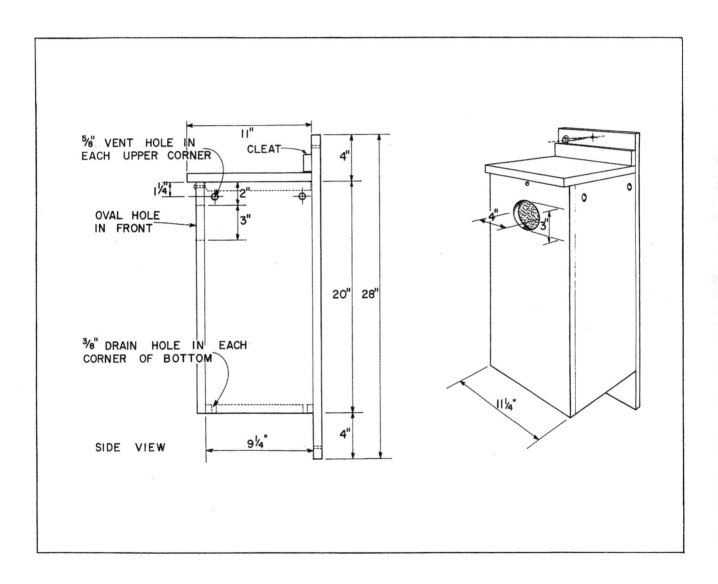

HOUSES FOR CHICKADEES, TITMICE, NUTHATCHES

Chickadees, titmice and nuthatches are woodland birds, and houses intended for them should be located in wooded areas. These birds also prefer a more natural house; hence this design.

An inch or two of coarse sawdust in the bottom of the house will simulate wood chips in a natural cavity and make the house more attractive.

Chickadees nest at low levels, so locate the house 3' to 10' above the ground for them. They also seem to prefer a house constructed from a birch log.

Titmice will use houses located 6' to 10' above the ground. Nuthatches prefer houses 10' to 20' above the ground. Attach houses to tree trunks in spots where they will be shaded by the foliage. The entrance hole should open to the east, south or west, away from the prevailing winter winds, because the same birds will use the houses for shelter during the winter.

RUSTIC HOUSE FOR CHICKADEES, TITMICE AND NUTHATCHES

MATERIALS

1 section, 6" × 13 inches to 16 inches, of a tree trunk or branch. (Birch, pine, cedar or basswood preferred)
1 piece 1 × 8 (about 3/4" × 7¼") × 8" or exterior plywood for roof
1 piece 1 × 6 (about 3/4" × 5½") × 5" or exterior plywood for bottom
8   1¾" or 2¼" nails. Use 4 for the sides and 4 for the floor
3   1¼" #10 roundhead wood screws to attach roof
1¼" × 2½" lag screw and washer for mounting

CONSTRUCTION

1. Cut block to overall length.
2. Split with axe or saw.
3. Cut front half to length.
4. Cut and split part of the back off so part is even with the front half and the remaining portion is about 1″ thick.

5. Use hammer or mallet and chisel to split out center to make a 4″ diameter tubular hollow.
6. Drill entrance hole and hole for lag screw and cut ventilation notches.
7. Nail halves together and attach roof and floor.

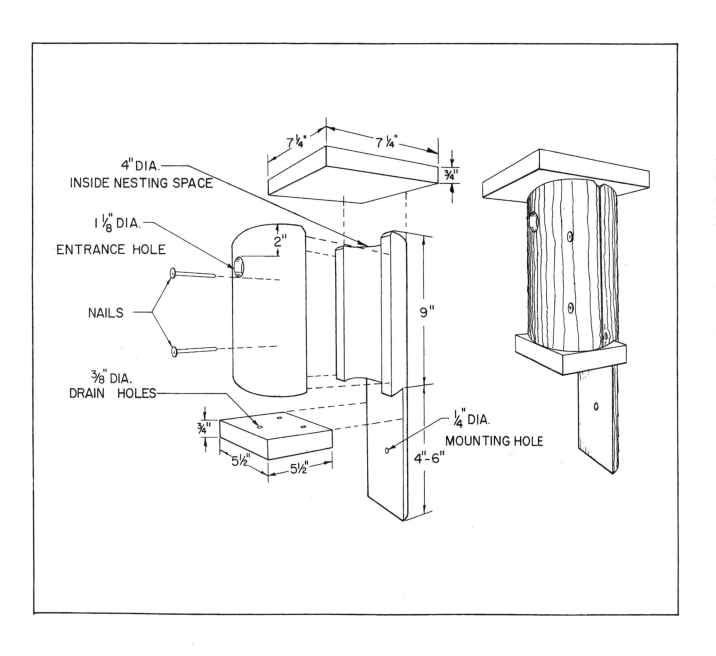

HOUSES FOR FOX AND GRAY SQUIRRELS

Tree squirrels such as the fox and gray squirrels readily use man-made houses. In areas lacking den trees, these houses can help to increase squirrel populations.

The squirrel house is identical to the wood duck house except for the size and location of the entrance hole and location of ventilation holes. Drill the vent holes on the side opposite the entrance. A smooth inside surface below the entrance hole is permissible.

Place houses at least 20' above the ground in trees that are at least 10" in diameter. The entrance hole should face south or east—away from prevailing winter winds—because squirrels will utilize houses not only for raising a family, but also for winter shelter.

The house can be half filled with dry leaves to make it more attractive to squirrels.

Houses in dense woods will be more apt to attract gray squirrels. Houses in open stands and on woods edges will probably attract fox squirrels.

One or two houses per acre in a woodland is usually sufficient to achieve a maximum squirrel population.

MOUNTING

Attach to tree trunk 20' to 30' above the ground. Use a lag screw and washer at both top and bottom of back piece.

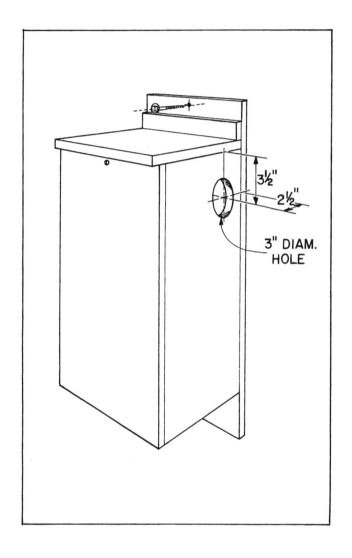

3½"
2½"
3" DIAM. HOLE

BAT CONSERVATION INTERNATIONAL'S OFFICIAL BAT HOUSE

More and more people are requesting information about bats and how to attract them. We hope this reflects a better public understanding of bats and bat ecology.

Bats respond to man-made housing in much the same way as birds. Unfortunately, they also respond to our houses and other buildings if access is available. The result is often an unwanted bat "infestation". If this is your problem, a bat house probably won't lure them away from your attic or barn. Bat proofing *is* the answer. For more information obtain UW–Extension Bulletin G3096, *Bats: Information for Wisconsin Homeowners.* Although a bat house will not solve a bat problem, it can attract bats to your yard where you can enjoy their magnificent flying skills and benefit from their insectivorous appetites.

The following design and instructions were provided by Bat Conservation International, a large conservation group dedicated to bats and worldwide bat conservation. If you want more information on bats and the activities of Bat Conservation International, write to BCI at PO Box 162603, Austin, Texas 78716.

The Little Brown Bat and the Big Brown Bat are most likely to use a bat house in Wisconsin.

To maximize your chances of attracting them, place your bat house 12' to 15' above the ground, and firmly attach it to the side of a building or a convenient tree. Sites near water are the most attractive. Try to shelter the bat house from prevailing winds. Bats are very temperature-sensitive and generally select stable temperatures between 80 and 100 degrees F. In our climate a sunny exposure will help maintain warm temperatures. A black roof on the house will also help.

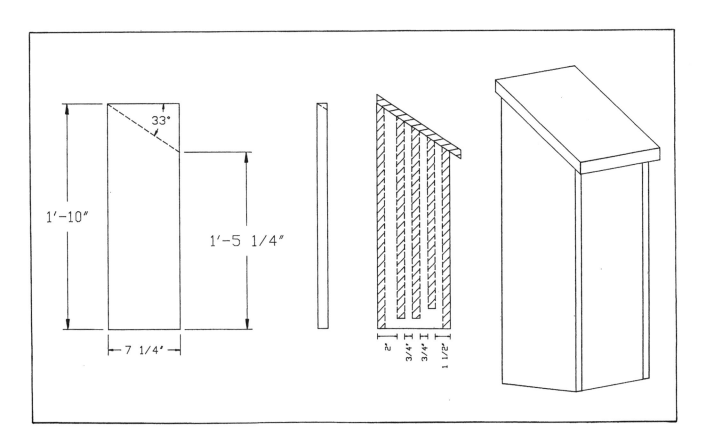

MATERIALS

1 piece 1 × 8 (about 3/4″ × 7¼″) × 12′ untreated,
   rough-sided cedar
1 piece 1 × 10 (about 3/4″ × 9¼″) × 11″ untreated,
rough-sided cedar for the top
about 20 6d galvanized nails

Tools:

   Skil saw with crosscut blade
   hammer
   ruler
   tape measure
   pencil

NOTES

1. Do not paint the sides or interior—the odor might repel bats.

2. Bats need a rough surface to secure a foothold. Be sure that all surfaces, especially those on the interior, are rough. If rough-sawn cedar is unavailable, roughen the boards by hand.

3. Some types of lumber split easily. You can avoid this by drilling small holes for the nails.

CONSTRUCTION

1. Cut the 12-foot cedar board into the following lengths:
   a) 3 pieces 22″ (for two sides and the back)
   b) 1 piece 17¼″ (for the front)
   c) 2 pieces 13″ (for two of the three partitions)
   d) 1 piece 11″ (for the final partition)

2. Take two of the 22″ pieces and measure off 17¼″ on one side of each piece. Make a pencil mark at this point.

3. Draw a diagonal line from the mark to the closest corner on the other side of the board.

4. Repeat Step 3 on the second piece.

5. Using a Skil saw, cut along the diagonal lines. Set these pieces aside for the moment (these will be the sides).

6. Adjust your Skil saw to a 33 degree angle. Take the third 22″ board (the one you didn't mark a diagonal line on) and angle off one of the ends. This piece will be the back of the box. Repeat the same for the front piece, top piece and the two partitions.

7. Take the two side pieces from Step 5 and, using a ruler and pencil, mark *both* pieces according to the measurements shown in this figure. Mark both sides of both boards.

8. You're ready to start building. Take the two sides, the 22″ back, and the 17¼″ front and nail them together as illustrated, angled ends up.

   *Note that the side pieces fit over the ends of the front and back pieces.

9. Insert the partitions. Lay the partially completed house on its side. Take the 13″ internal partition and slide it into the box, *centering* it along the set of pencil lines closest to the back of the box. Position the partition so that it is flush with the tops of the sides.

10. Nail the partition in place from the outside. Use the outside lines as a guide for nail placement.

11. Follow the same procedure to nail both of the shorter partitions along the other two sets of lines near the front of the box.

12. Place the 10-inch 1 × 10 board on top so that its back edge is flush with the back of the box and creates an overhang in the front and on the sides. Hold firmly and nail the top to the main frame. The completed house should look like the drawing on the left.

FEEDERS

Feeding song birds is rapidly becoming a national pastime. It is the simplest way to bring a variety of birds within easy viewing distance.

Bird feeding is most effective during the winter months, but some birds will use feeders periodically throughout the year if they are kept supplied with food. Keep in mind, though, that summer feeding can cause problems. Summer temperatures facilitate the spread of disease. Mourning doves are especially susceptible to a disease called trichomoniasis. If doves use your feeder, remove all feed and clean the feeder throughly in spring and discontinue feeding until cool weather returns. Natural food is usually abundant during summer, but specialized feeders—a syrup feeder for hummingbirds, for example—can bring fascinating birds into view.

Except for hummingbirds, birds using feeders are of two general types: the seed eaters, such as sparrows, finches and grosbeaks; and the insect or meat eaters, such as chickadees, nuthatches, woodpeckers and titmice. To attract the greatest variety of bird life we must provide suitable food for each of these groups. The insect or meat eaters like suet, while the seed eaters like a variety of seeds. These two types of food, seeds and suet, get best results with feeders designed to handle each kind. Therefore, several different feeder designs are included in this publication.

Many commercial seed mixes are available, but some contain large amounts of seeds that most birds do not prefer. Most mixes can be improved by adding more sunflower seeds. Research has shown that small, black "oil-type" sunflower seeds are superior to large, gray, striped ones. They are the best buy for your bird-feeding dollar. White proso millet and cracked corn are also economical, and popular with birds. Many local Audubon Society chapters and nature centers are excellent sources of good quality seed.

Some birds have very specific seed preferences. You can easily attract these birds by feeding some special seeds in addition to mixes. Goldfinches, for example, readily come to niger thistle seed, and cardinals are fond of safflower seeds. These and other special seeds are expensive and may require special feeders.

The effectiveness of a total feeding program is often determined not so much by the design of the feeder as by its location. Winter feeders should be situated where they are protected from strong winds, and preferably near shrubbery or conifers where the birds can take shelter. Several feeders are often more effective than a single feeder in a backyard because they give more birds an opportunity to feed at the same time.

Be careful that feeders are not located near a spot where a cat can hide. Also, be prepared to tolerate or deal with squirrels. Squirrels can be interesting visitors to feeders—their antics are often fun to watch—but they can monopolize feeders. If this happens, place squirrel guards on feeder poles, place the feeder away from trees squirrels can jump from, buy a "squirrel-proof" feeder (several of those available commercially do seem to work) or catch the offending squirrels in a live trap and move them to the countryside.

To be really effective, a winter feeding program should be started early—in late October or November—and must be continued without interruption into spring. Birds develop feeding patterns, and interruptions in the food supply may cause them to abandon feeders.

Many excellent books on bird feeders and feeding are available. We recommend further reading if you plan to take up bird feeding seriously.

SHELTERED FEEDER

MATERIALS

Enough 1/2" exterior plywood for 1 piece 2' × 4' and
 1 piece 1' × 2' each with grain on the face ply in
 the 2' direction
Waterproof glue
1¼" nails
Window screen to cover drain holes

MOUNTING

Attach to steel fence post with bolts through the back. Attach to wood post with lag screw through bottom into top of post. Balance feeder on top of post to determine center of gravity.

WINDOW SILL FEEDER

MATERIALS

For bottom: 1/2" or 3/4" exterior plywood or 1 × 12
 lumber (about 3/4" × 11¼")
For edge: 5/16" × 1¾" lattice or 1/4" plywood strips
1" or 1¼" nails
Waterproof glue
3' small-link brass or galvanized chain
4 screw eyes or screw hooks
Window screen to cover drain holes

MOUNTING

The south side of the house will provide some protection from prevailing winter winds.

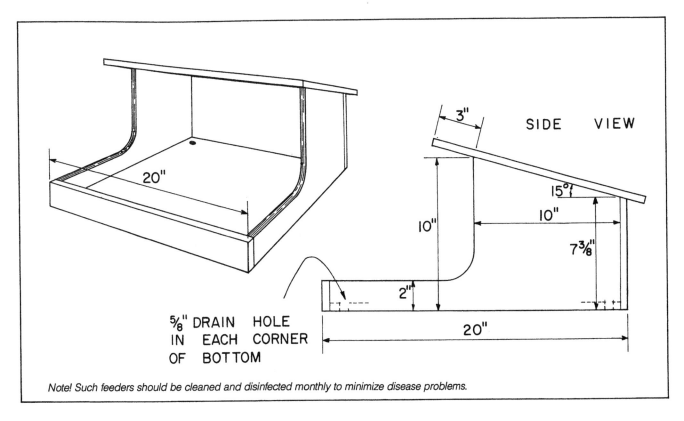

5⁄8" DRAIN HOLE
IN EACH CORNER
OF BOTTOM

Note! Such feeders should be cleaned and disinfected monthly to minimize disease problems.

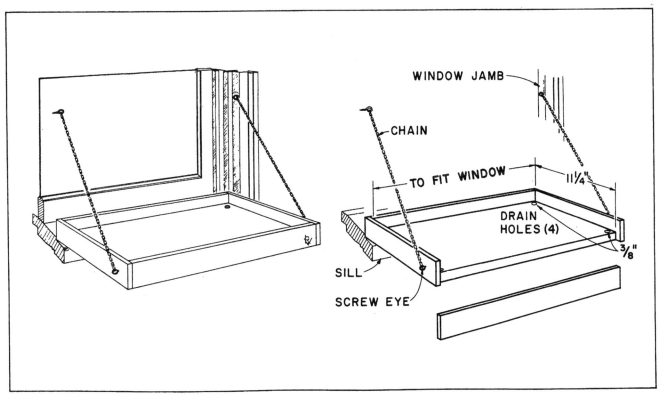

LOG SUET FEEDER

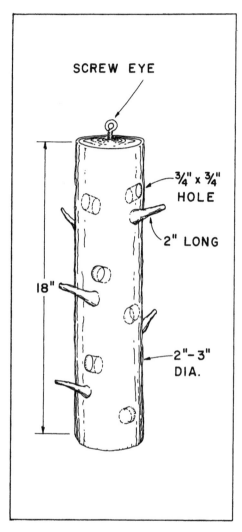

SCREW EYE

¾" × ¾"
HOLE

2" LONG

18"

2"–3"
DIA.

Hang from a low branch of a tree for easy refilling.

SUET FEEDER

MATERIALS

1 piece 1 × 10 (about 3/4″ × 9¼″) × 2′, or 3/4″
    exterior grade plywood equivalent
1 piece 5/16″ to 1/2″ lattice 3′ long for strips to hold
    hardware cloth in place
1 piece 7½″ × 8″ hardware cloth, 1/3″ mesh
1 pair 1″ × 1″ butt hinges with screws
1¼″ nails or 1″ flat head wood screws to attach strips
1¾″ or 2¼″ nails for general assembly
Waterproof glue

MOUNTING

Use roundhead or lag screws, etc., attach to post, tree
or building, 5′ to 6′ above the ground. If possible,
select a location sheltered from the north and west
winds.

CIRCULAR FEEDER

MATERIALS

1 piece 3/4″ exterior plywood 2′ × 2′
7 screw eyes
2′ small-link brass or galvanized chain
1¼″ wire nails
Waterproof glue

CONSTRUCTION

1″ guard rail may be attached to the 10″ diameter bottom piece by either nails or waterproof glue. The same
applies to the two roof pieces.

MOUNTING

Hang from a low branch of a tree so it can be reached
for easy refilling.

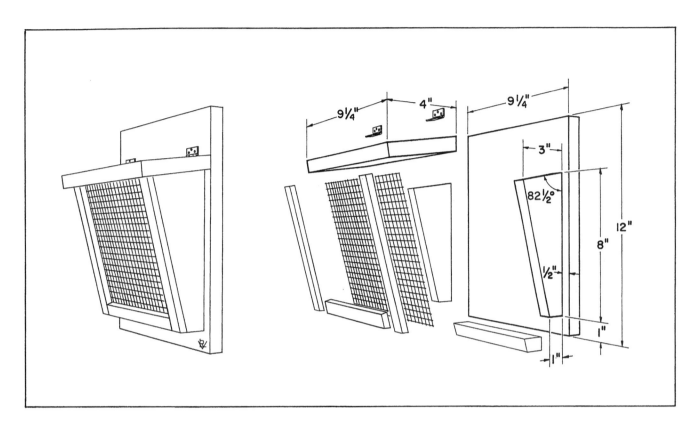

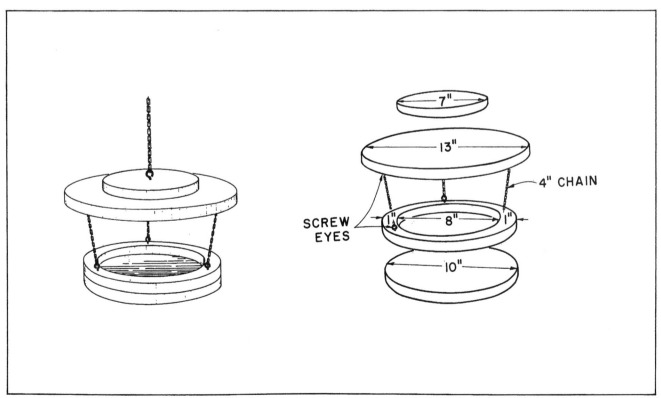

TIN CAN FEEDER

MATERIALS

1 piece 1 × 8 (about 3/4″ × 7¼″) × 16″ board or
  3/4″ × 8″ × 16″ exterior plywood
1 piece 1/4″ × 1/4″ × 16″
1 piece 1/4″ × 1 3/8″ × 33″ lattice
1 fruit juice can about 4¼″ × 7″
42″ #16, 17 or 18 wire
3/4″ wire nails

FINISH FOR FRUIT JUICE CAN

Wash can with vinegar, allow to dry, then wash with
clean water and allow to dry. Paint with a good grade
of exterior house paint, metal paint or enamel. Use
metal primer if available.

MOUNTING

Hang from a low branch of a tree so it can be reached
for easy refilling.

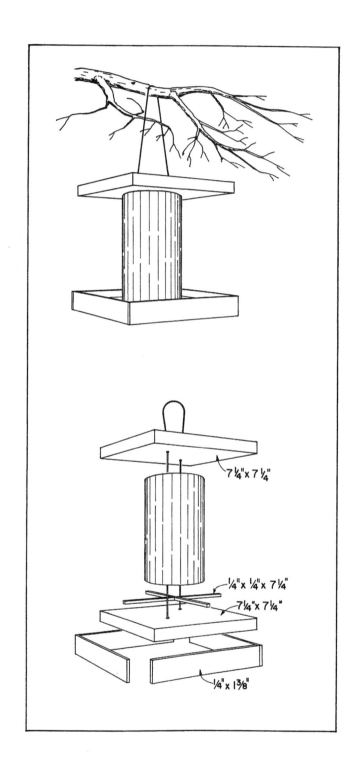

7¼″ x 7¼″

¼″x ¼″x 7¼″

7¼″x 7¼″

¼″ x 1⅜″

RECYCLING FOR FEEDERS AND HOUSES

There is more than one way to recycle.

Many household items that often wind up in the landfill can be recycled into wildlife homes and feeders. Recycling for wildlife is fun, effective, and inexpensive!

This section suggests uses for soda bottles, buckets, milk jugs and cartons, and old tires. Use your imagination to come up with other new uses for household trash. Remember to locate and care for recycled feeders and houses just as you would traditional or commercial designs.

MILK JUG OR BLEACH BOTTLE FEEDERS

MATERIALS

1/2 gallon or gallon jug
small dowels or sticks
hanging cord

CONSTRUCTION

First, be certain the jug is completely clean. Cut two or three holes several inches above the bottom of the jug. Size of the holes (from 2″ to 4″ diameter) depends on birds you wish to attract. Insert a dowel or stick below each hole as a perch. Fill to hole level with seed and hang in a convenient tree or shrub.

CARDBOARD MILK OR JUICE CARTON FEEDER

Cut a notch out of the container, fill and hang.

Note: NEVER use plastic bottles or jugs for bird housing. They overheat very quickly.

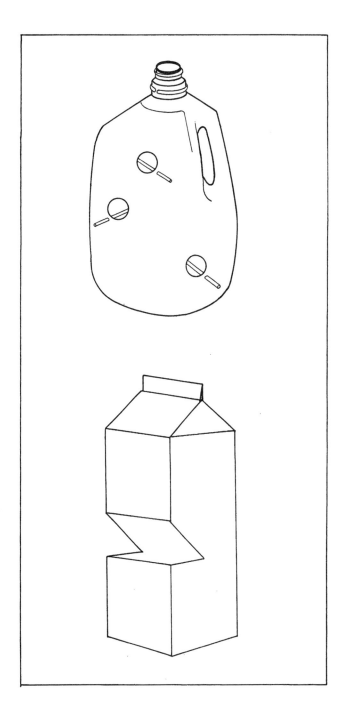

SUNFLOWER/SAFFLOWER SEED FEEDER

MATERIALS

Three 2-liter plastic soda bottles
7″ dessert topping lid
baby-food jar lid
coping saw
single-edged razor blade or "X-acto" knife
all-weather rubber or silicone sealant
8 inches of wire or monofilament fishing line
small nail or 7/16″ bit and hand drill
metal or wood screw

Soak a 2-liter bottle in warm, soapy water. Remove label and rinse. Pull off the colored plastic base and save it for measuring when you cut the feeding holes.

CONSTRUCTION

1. On another 2-liter bottle, make a perpendicular cut with the coping saw at the bottle's mouth down to the point at which the neck collar begins. Make a second cut at and slightly above the collar, perpendicular to the first cut. Discard the cut piece. Cut the rest of the neck and collar away from the bottle, leaving at least a 1″ flange of plastic beneath the collar. Using a third 2-liter bottle, repeat these steps. You now have two spouts to use as feeding holes. Their neck pieces will prevent seed spillage.

2. Cut two 1″ circular holes across from each other in the sides of the first bottle. Using the top of the plastic base as a guide, make the top of each cut at the same point as the top of the plastic base.

3. Apply sealant around the outside of each feeding hole. Insert the spouts into the bottle, flange end outward. The collar on each spout and the sealant will form a watertight gasket. Secure with a rubber band until dry.

4. Using the drill or small nail, make small holes in the bottom of the bottle and the dessert-topping and baby-food lids. Attach the two lids, with the baby food lid on the bottom, to the bottom of the bottle with the metal or wood screw. The topping lid forms a perch that the baby-food lid will stabilize.

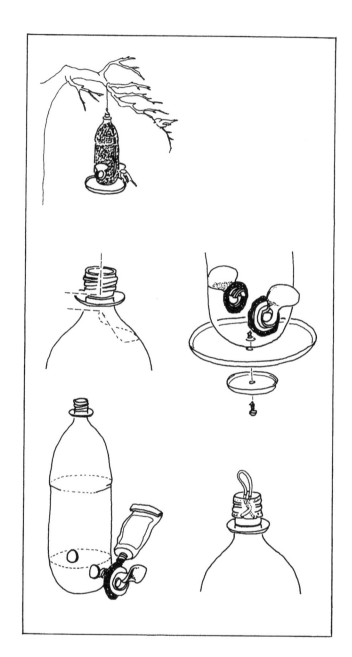

5. Drill or punch two small, parallel holes in the bottle top. String wire or monofilament line through the holes and tie. Fill the bottle with sunflower seeds, then screw the top onto the bottle.

MOUNTING

Hang the feeder in a tree or from a pole where it can be easily filled, seen from a window, and conveniently used by birds.

THISTLE SEED FEEDER

MATERIALS

1- or 2-liter plastic soda bottle
three or four 3/16″ wide, 5″ long wooden dowels
   (straight hardwood sticks will do)
a single-edged razor blade or "X-acto" knife
8 inches of wire or monofilament fishing line
one metal eye screw
hand drill and small bit

Soak the bottle in warm, soapy water. Remove label and rinse. Pull off the colored plastic base and discard.

CONSTRUCTION

1. Make small parallel cuts in each side of the bottle with the razor blade, "X-acto" knife, or hand drill. Insert the dowels as perches. Alternate the radial alignment of each perch so that all sides of the bottle are used.

2. At points about one inch below each dowel, make small 1/4″ long, 1/8″ wide incisions through the bottle for feeding holes. Don't make the cuts too large—the correct size will allow birds to pick out individual seeds yet prevent spillage. (A wood-burning needle will also make the right-sized feeding holes.)

3. Bore a 7/16″ hole in the bottom of the bottle and insert the eye screw. When suspended, the bottom becomes the top of the feeder. Affix wire or monofilament line to the eye screw and tie.

MOUNTING

Hang the feeder in a tree or from a pole where it can be easily filled, seen from a window, and conveniently used by birds.

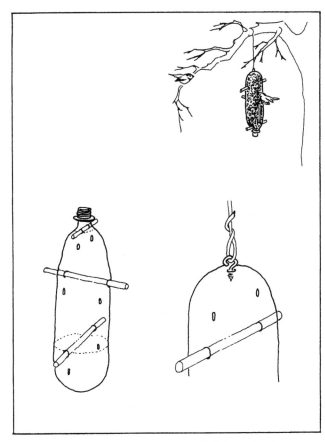

Pop bottle feeder plans courtesy of the U.S. Fish and Wildlife Service.

TIRE SHELTERS

The Maryland Game and Inland Fish Commission developed a design that uses one-half of a car tire to make a durable, weatherproof squirrel house. Squirrels seem to like them, and they are fairly inexpensive and vandal-proof. However, steel-belted radials do not work well due to the cutting involved.

MATERIALS

House—One 14″ to 16″ automobile tire (one tire will make two houses). Steel-belted radials are not recommended.

Hanger—Eighteen inches of sturdy, bendable metal rod.

Nails—Six 2″ galvanized roofing nails.

Washers—Seven roofing caps (six for the nails and one for the hanger).

Equipment—Carpet knife, electric jigsaw with knife-edge blades, electric drill with bits, pliers, cord with weight, rope, and metal tubing.

CONSTRUCTION

1. Remove both beads and cut the tire in half (Fig. 1a). You can use a modified hacksaw blade or linoleum or carpet knife if you're only cutting a few tires. Be careful when cutting tires with a carpet knife to pre-vent slips due to hand and wrist fatigue. If you have to cut a lot of tires, an electric jigsaw fitted with a knife-edge blade may prove handy. Drill starter holes for the jigsaw blade. The knife-edge blades tend to overheat and break, so plan on replacing blades after cutting five to 10 tires.

2. Make the cuts and drill the holes in each tire half as shown in Figure 1b. A carpet knife may give better control for making these small cuts.

3. Bend the lower end up and inside the upper end. Match the appropriate holes and fasten the sides together using the roofing nails. If you have trouble matching the sides, fold the tire and use the outer holes as guides to mark the inner holes.

4. Fasten holes so that the upper side overlaps the lower side to keep rain out (Fig. 1c).

5. Drill the hole for the hanger so that the entrance tilts slightly downward to exclude rain, and drill four or five 3/8″ to 1/2″ holes in the bottom of the house for drainage.

6. Bend one end of the hanger rod into a tight loop or crimp. Slide a roofing cap, followed by a 2″ x 2″ rubber square, down to this crimp. This will help prevent the hanger from pulling through the top.

7. Insert the rod through the top of the shelter and bend it to form an open loop to fit over a tree limb (Fig. 1c).

MOUNTING

Hang the shelter from a tree limb at least 15 feet up. Unless you're very sure of your tree-climbing abilities, use a ladder or sectional pole to hang it.

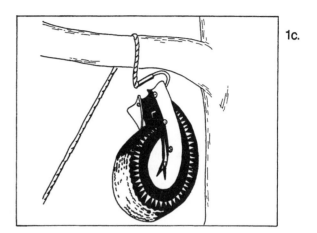

1a.

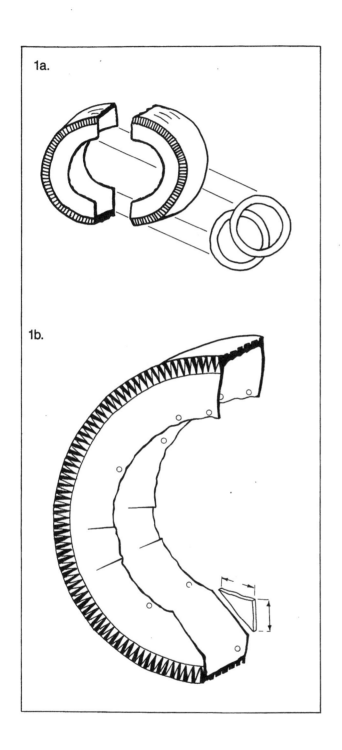

1b.

1c.

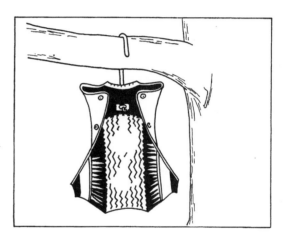

Instructions adapted from a Maryland Game and Inland Fish Commission brochure.

PLASTIC PAIL WOOD DUCK HOUSES

MATERIALS

2 five-gallon plastic pails
1 6″ × 14″ piece of 1/4″ mesh hardware cloth
2 Number 8-32 × 1/2″ machine screws with nuts
   and washers
1 1/2″ × 12″ pipe nipple
2 1/2″ pipe flanges
4 1/4″ × 3/4″ bolts with nuts and washers
3 1/2″ × 2″ lag bolts
2 lbs sawdust

CONSTRUCTION

1. Draw a line around what will be the bottom pail just
   below the handle brackets with a felt-tipped marker,
   and cut off the top portion. At least 9½ inches of
   the pail should remain.

2. Draw and cut out a 3″ × 4″ oval entrance hole on
   the side of the top pail, one inch above the bottom.
   The shape helps to keep out hungry raccoons.

3. Drill two 3/16″ holes in the side of the pail, 2½
   inches below the corners of the entrance hole and
   4½ inches apart.

4. Cut a piece of 1/4″ mesh hardware cloth six inches
   wide by 14 inches long. Trim all edges to eliminate
   sharp wires. Attach to inside of top pail, flush with
   bottom of entrance, using two number 8-32 × 1/2″
   machine screws, nuts and washers. This screen
   gives the ducklings a foothold for climbing out.

5. Position a 1/2″ pipe flange on back side of top pail,
   opposite entrance hole and about halfway up. Mark
   and drill four 1/4″ bolt holes. Bolt flange to pail
   using four 1/4″ × 3/4″ bolts, nuts and washers.

6. Drill four to six 3/8″ holes in the bottom of the pail
   for drainage and pour in 3 inches of sawdust.

7. Place the top pail over bottom pail and push
   together for a tight friction fit.

MOUNTING

Mount house on a tree about 6′ to 10′ feet above
ground. Anchor the 1/2″ pipe flange with three 1/4″ ×
2″ lag bolts and screw in 1/2″ × 12″ pipe nipple.
Remove top of house and thread flange to pipe.
Replace bottom of house.

You can also mount wood duck houses on 1¼″ to 2″
steel poles using two U-bolts attached to the back of
the top bucket as shown, one above the other. Not all
plastic pails are the same. If the two halves don't seem
to nest snugly enough, attach a piece of wire from one
handle-hole to the other, running it under the bottom
bucket.

Plastic pails come in a variety of colors—green, gray,
brown and white. To make them blend into the environ-
ment better—especially the white ones—you can
″camouflage″ them with enamel spray-paint. Let dry at
least one week to get rid of paint odor before mounting outdoors.

*Instructions adapted from ″Plastic Pail Condos for Wood Ducks″ by
William Meier, in Wisconsin Natural Resources Magazine.*

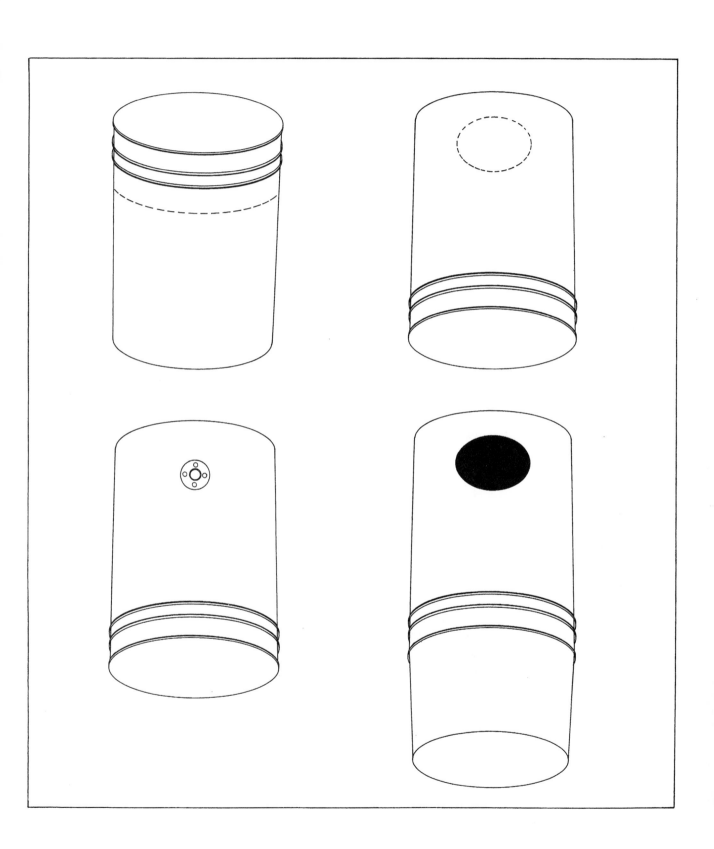